Adult Coloring Book: Great For Relaxing, Reducing Stress, Calming Nerves And Comprehension Therapy

Filled With A Hodgepodge Of Food And Nature In Both Solids And Unique Patterns

Ayesha Moore

Description

An adult coloring book to help with relaxing and reducing stress. This book is set up with alternating patterns for relaxing concentration and quick stress relief. Perfect for idle hands and idle minds.

TITLE: BOOKSHELF

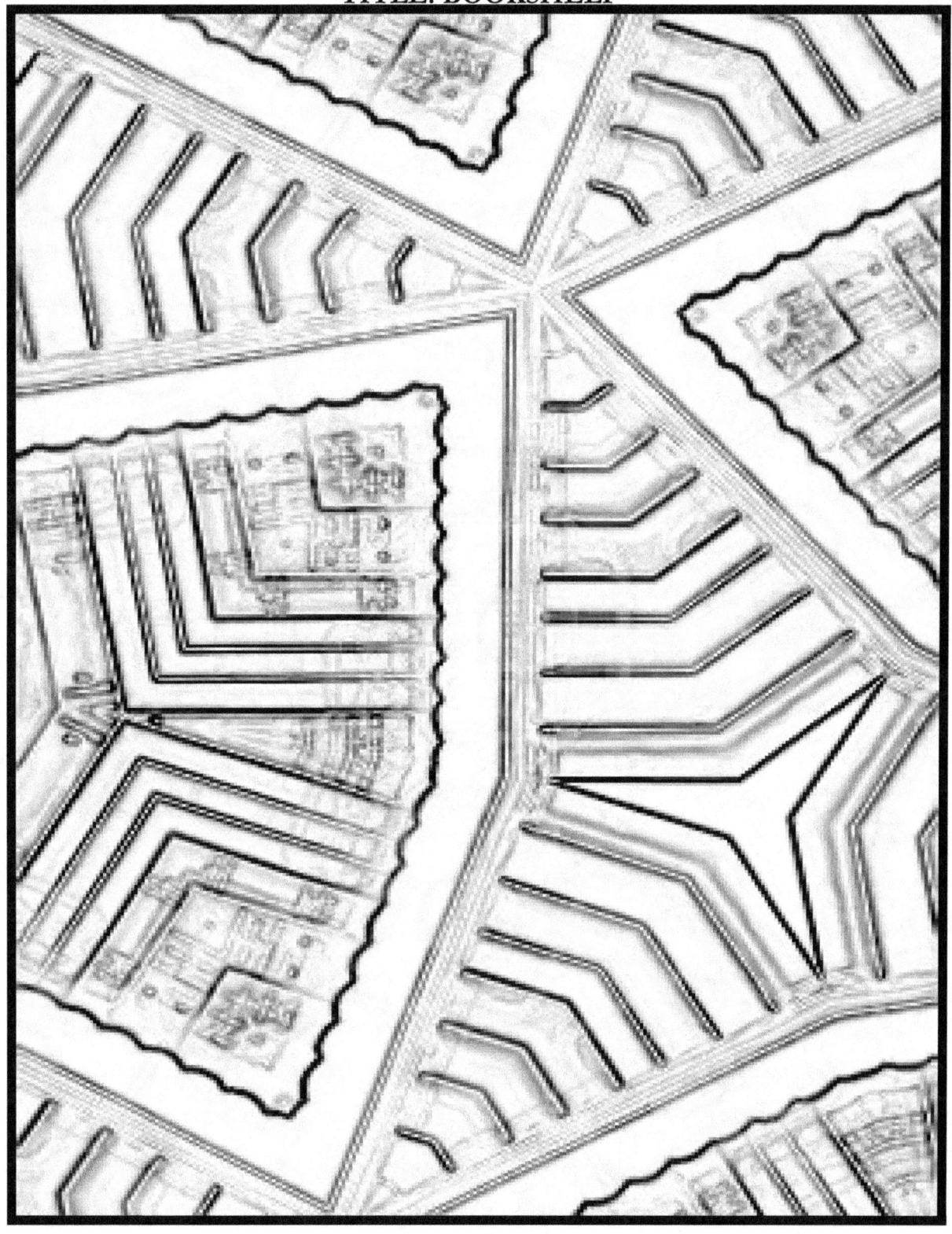

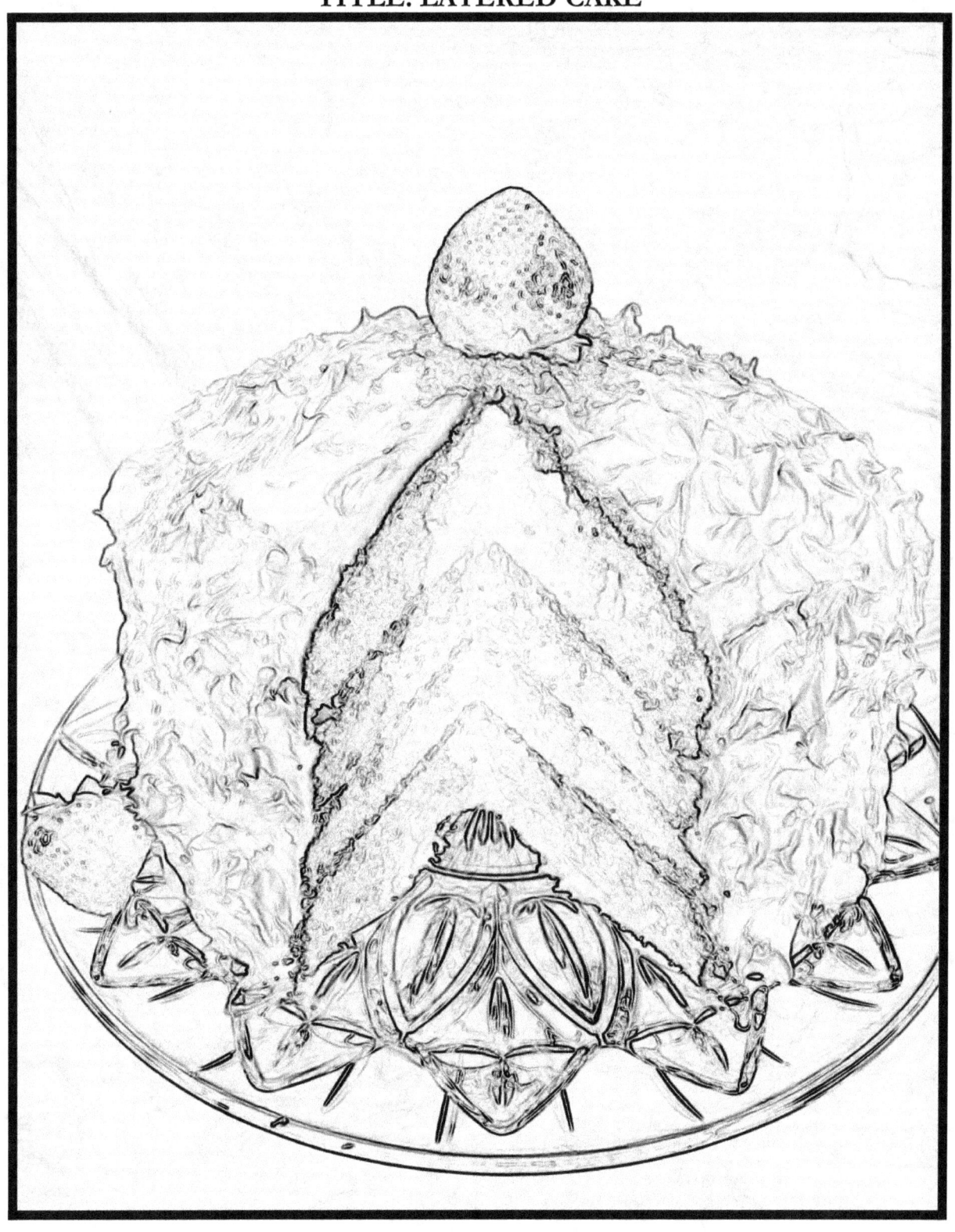

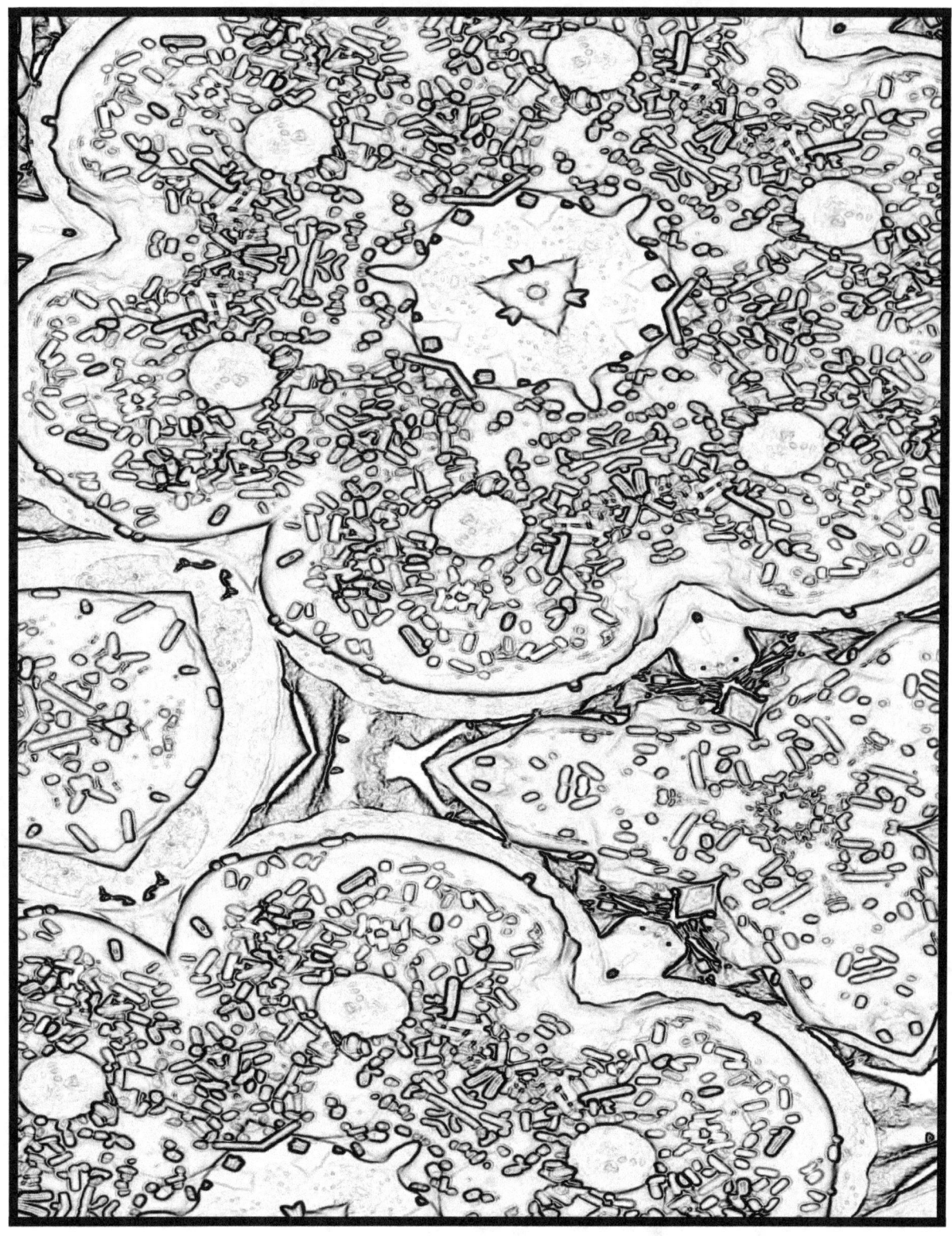

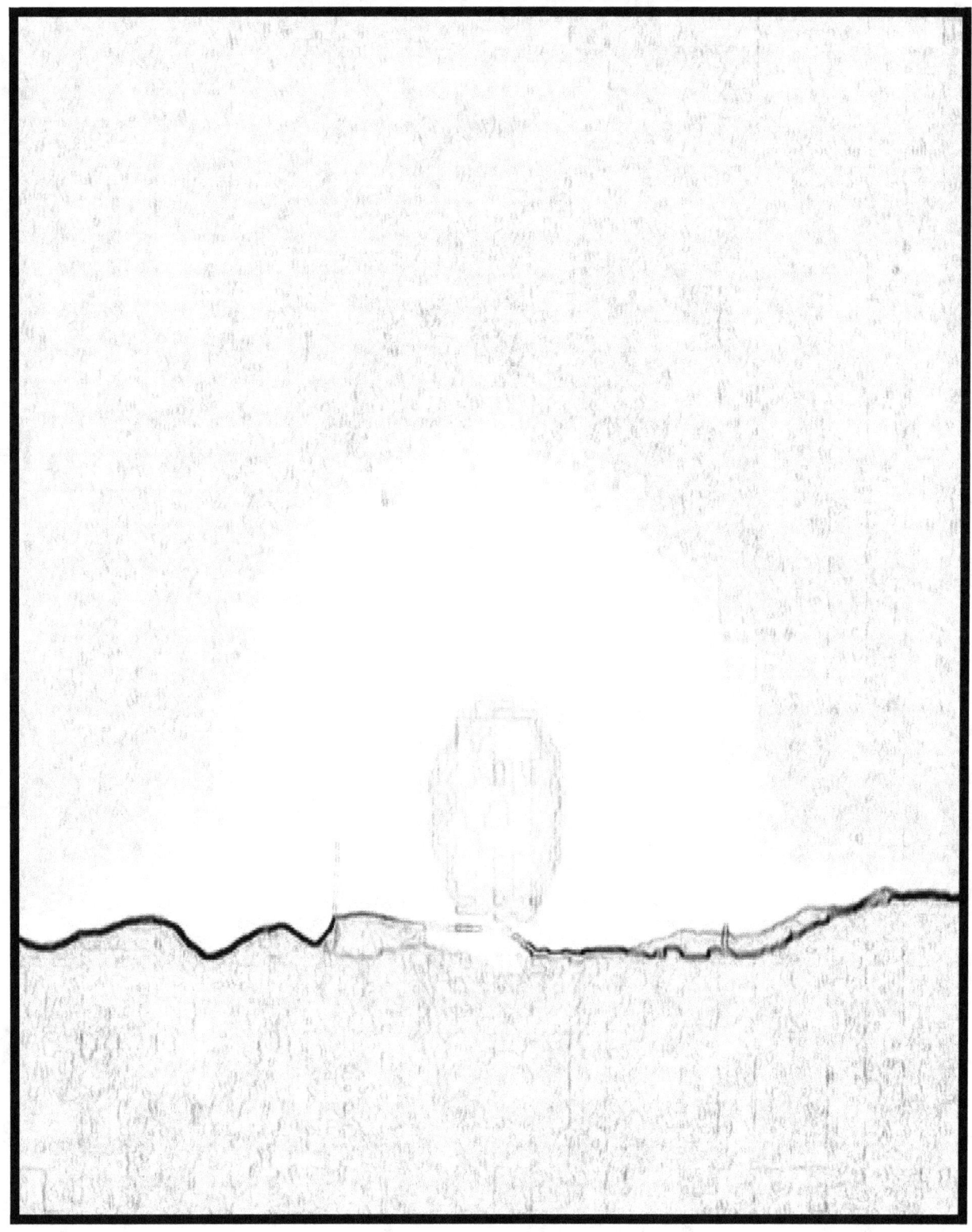

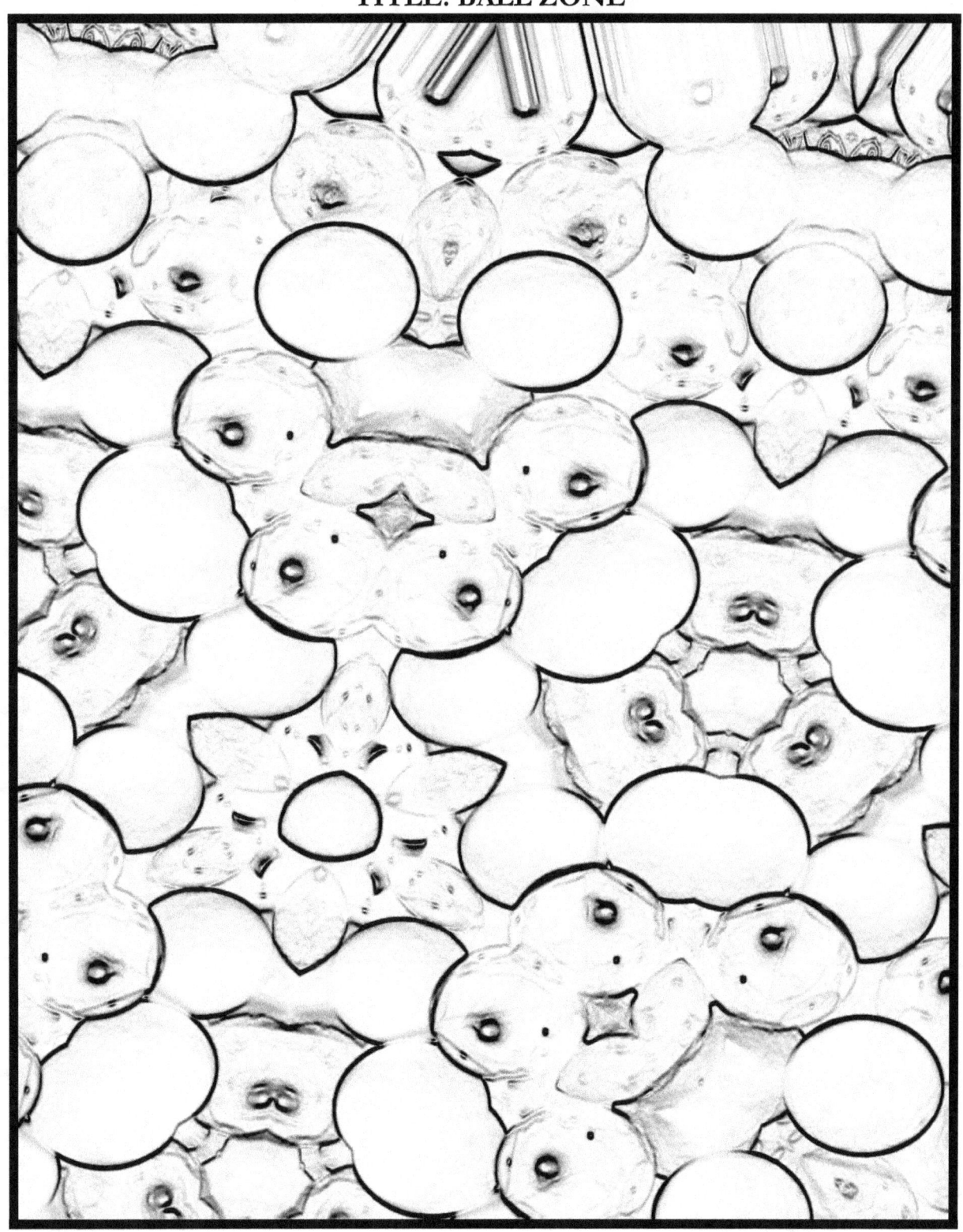

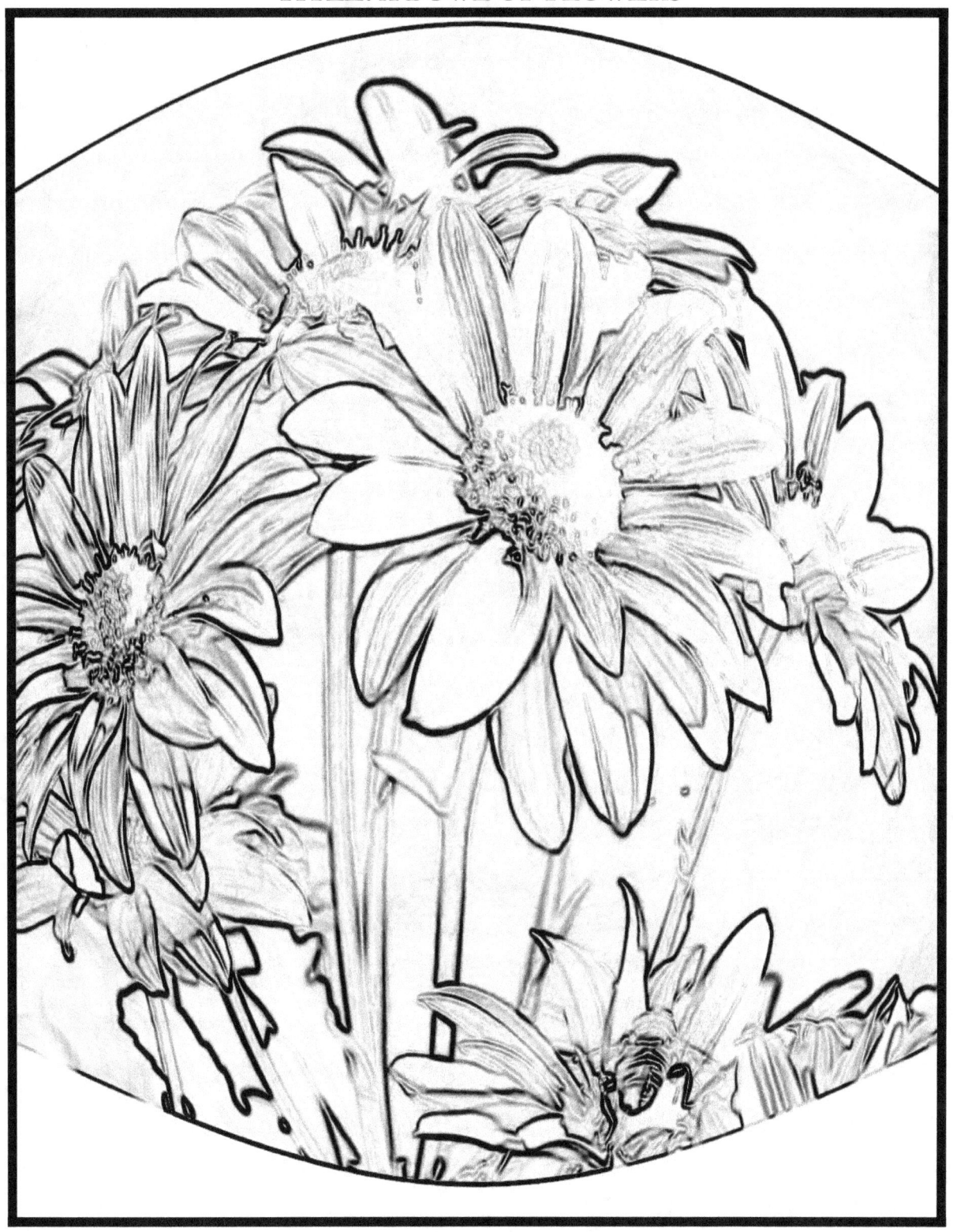

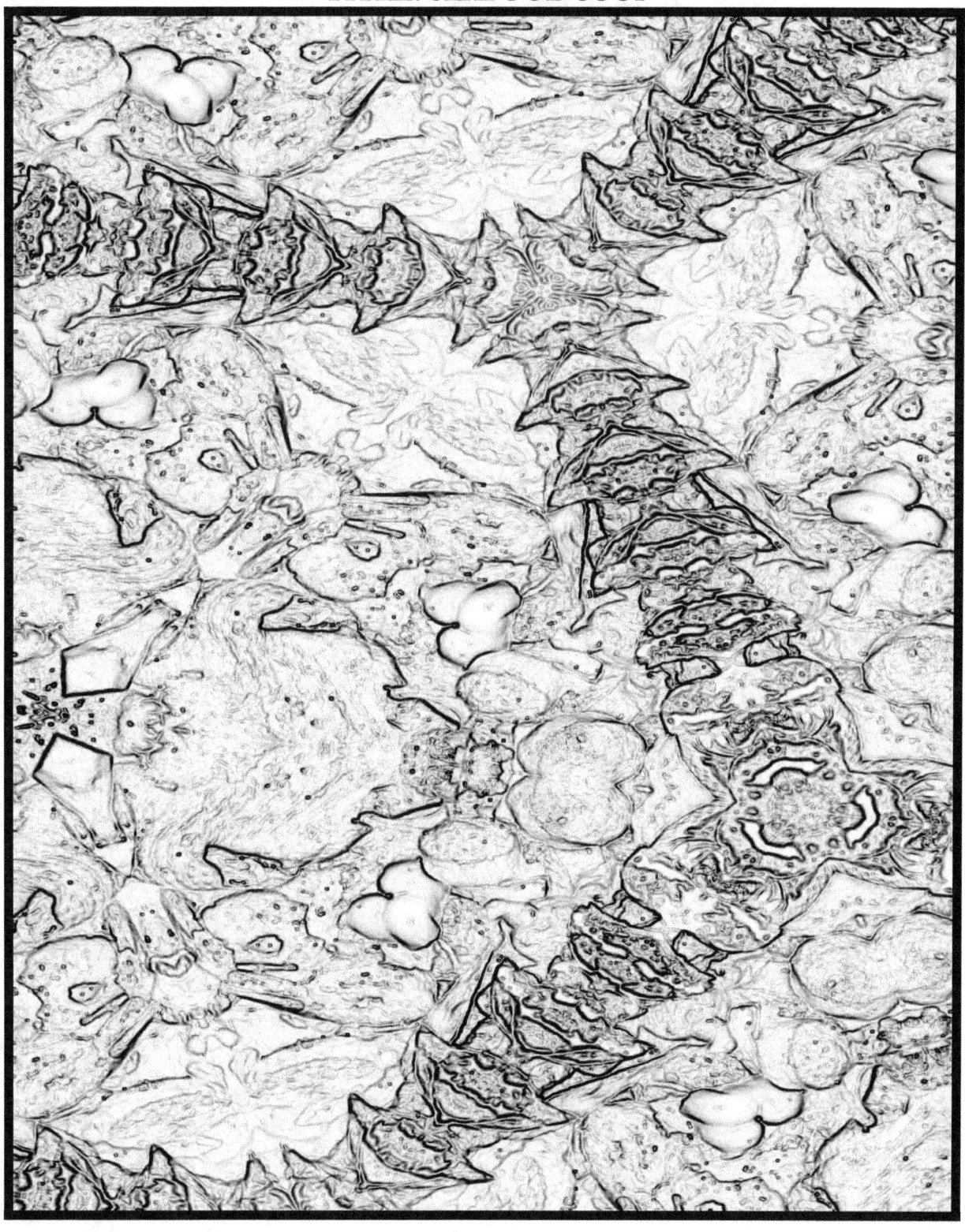

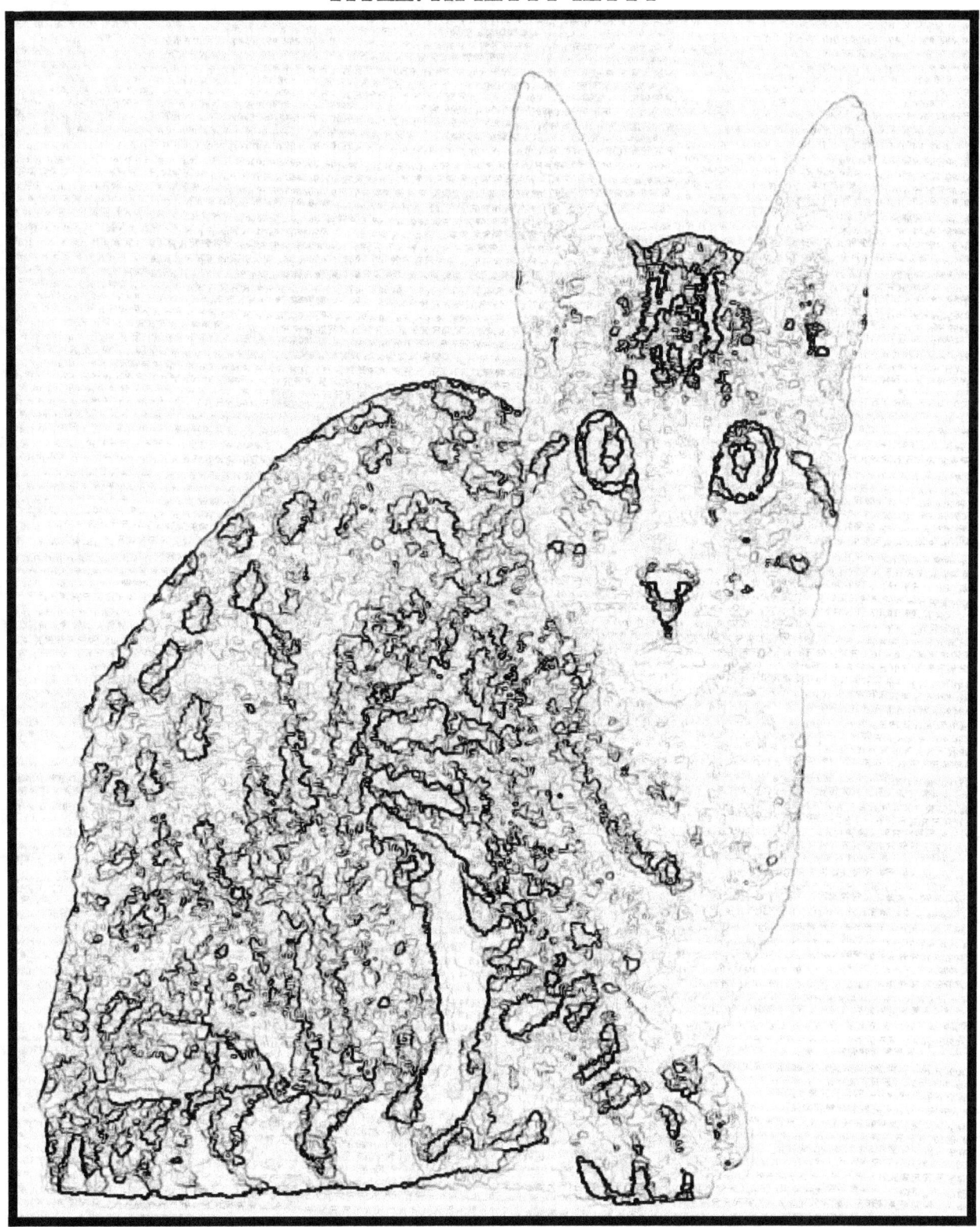

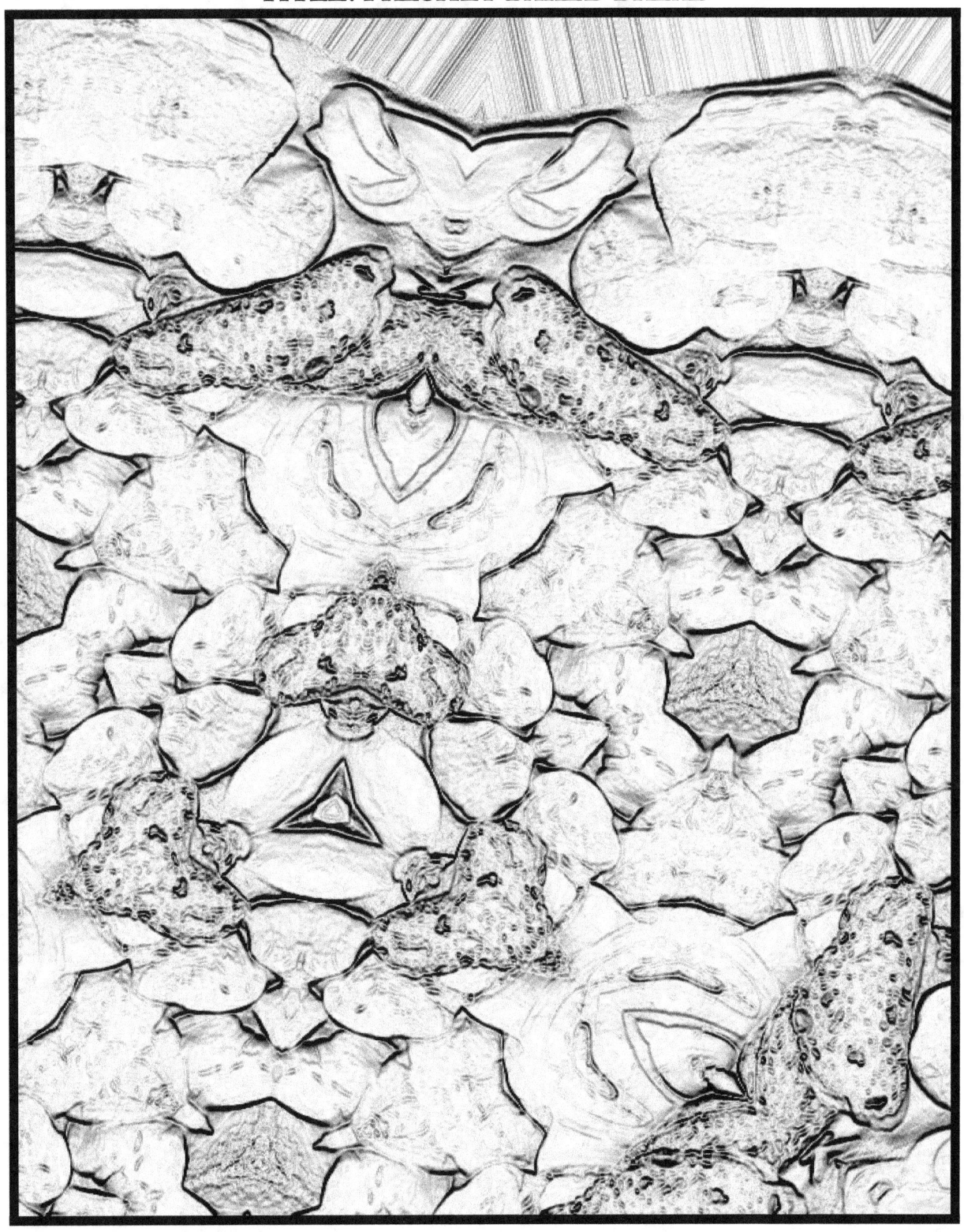

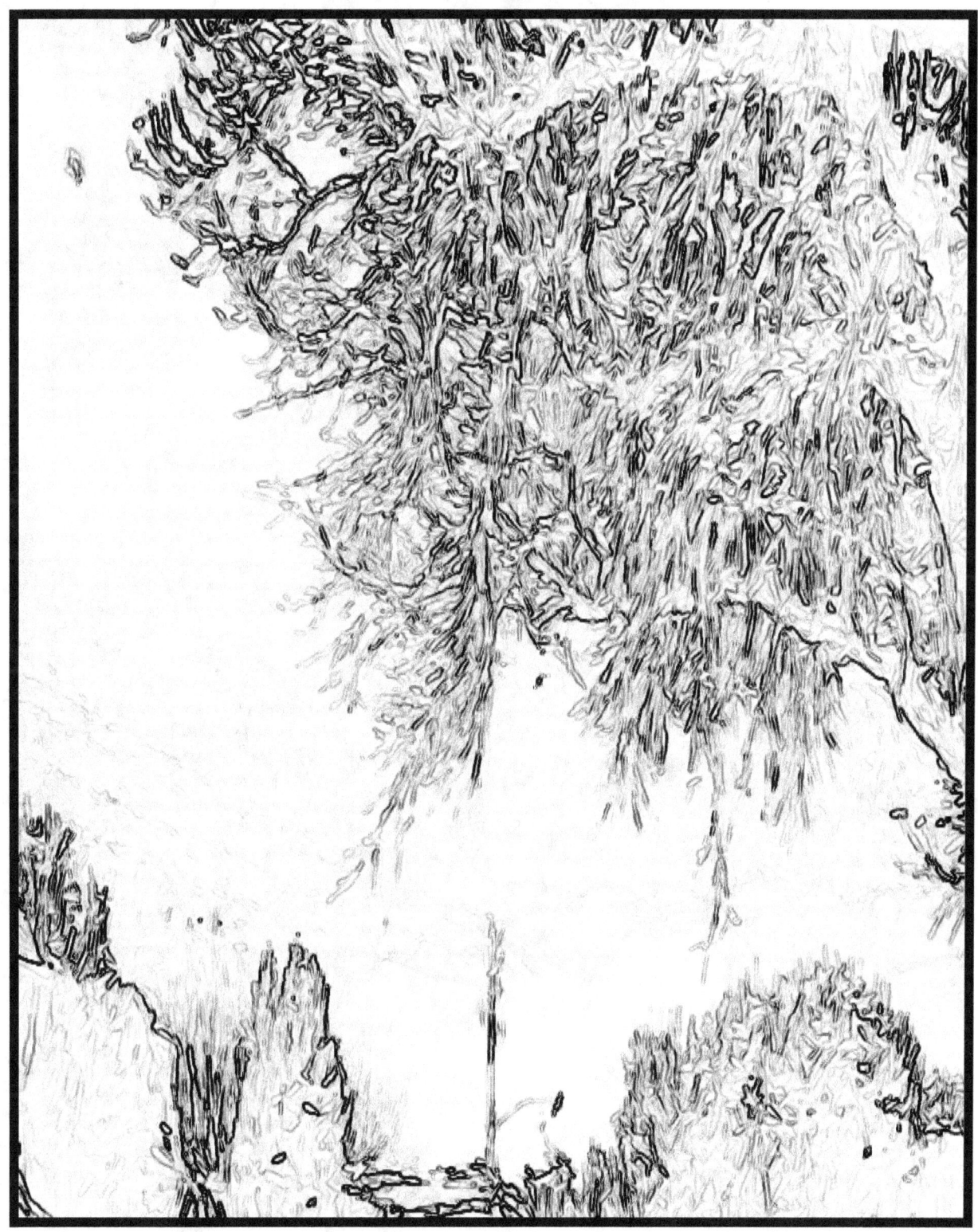

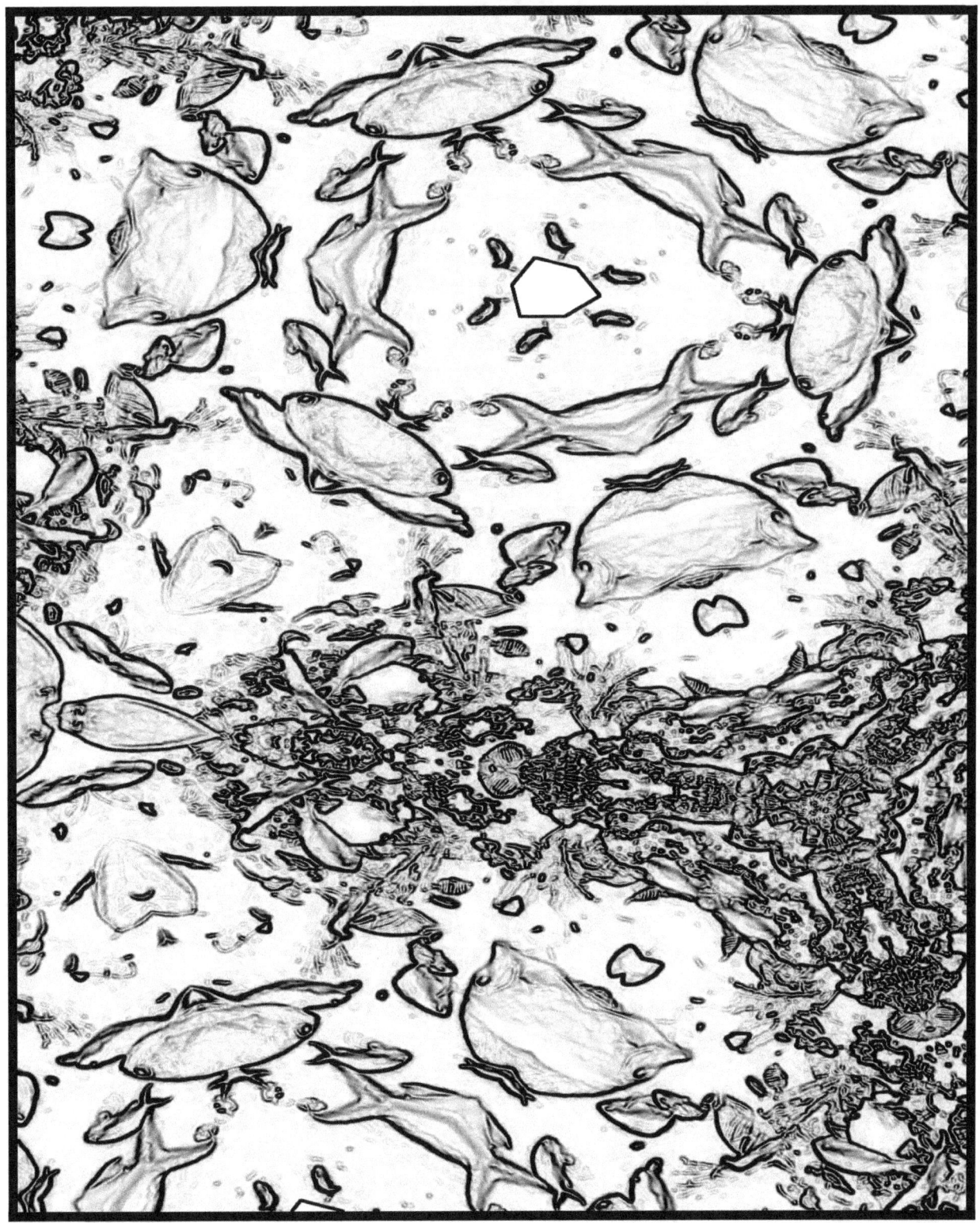

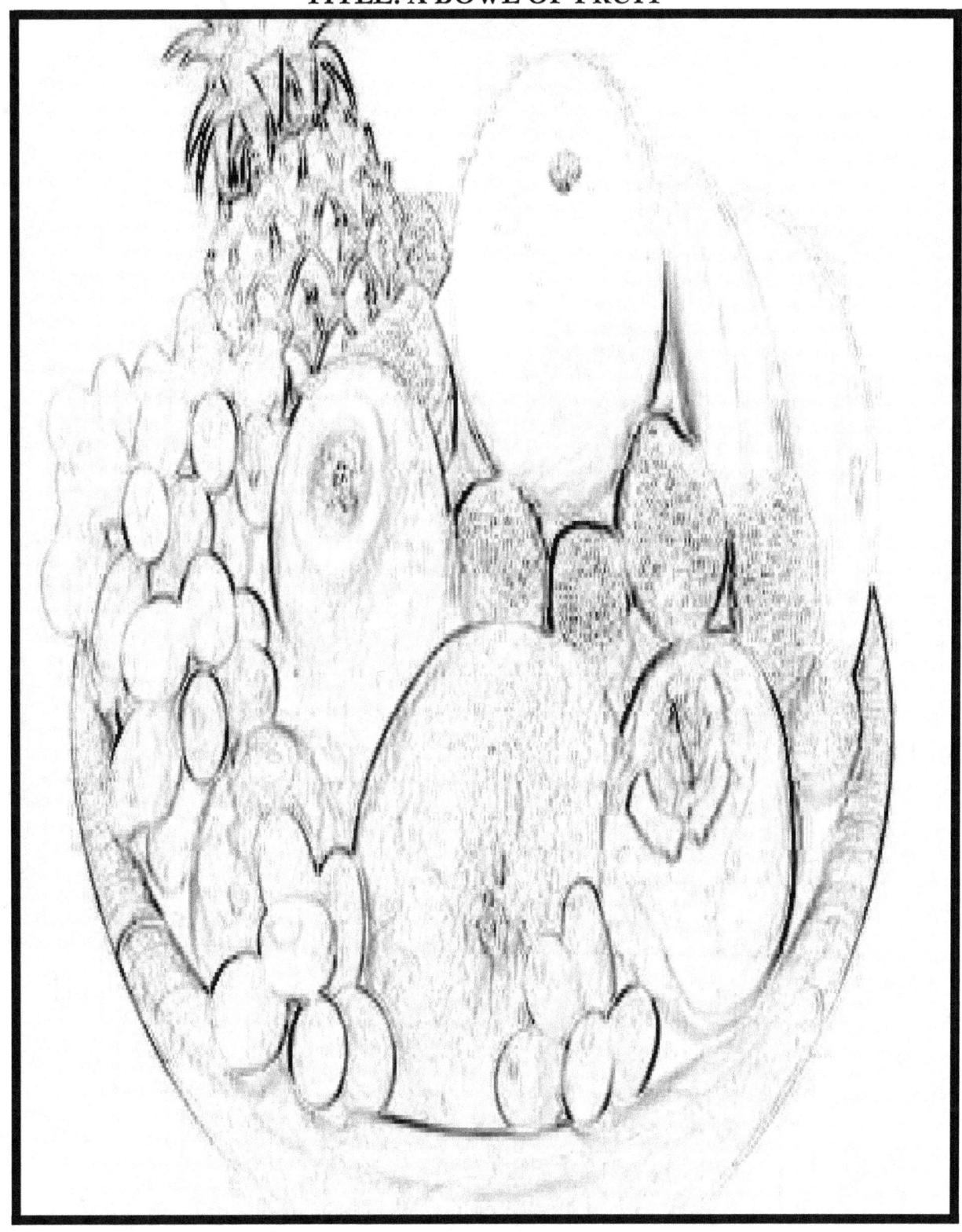

RELAX AND CONCENTRATE
TITLE: AMERICA

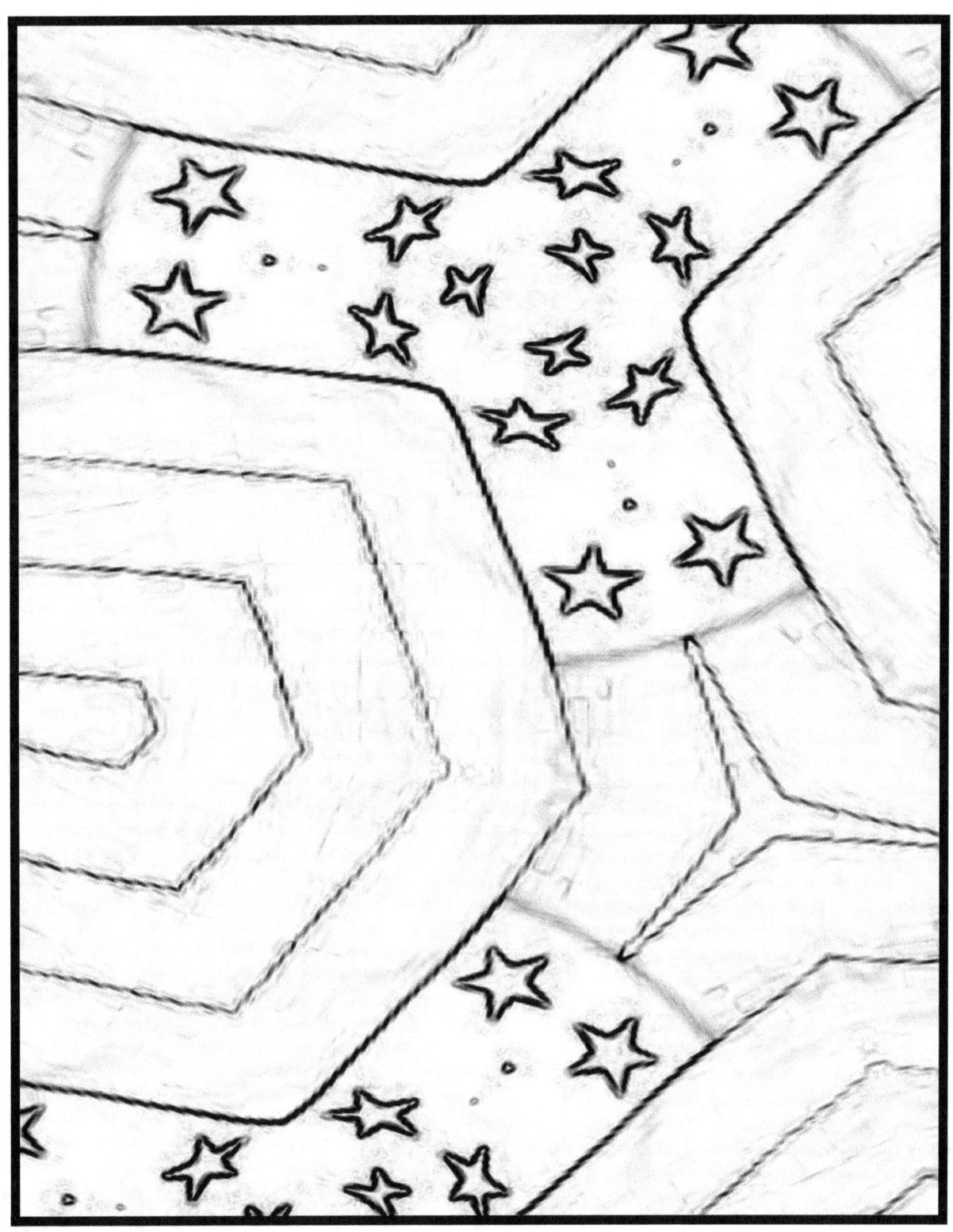

25

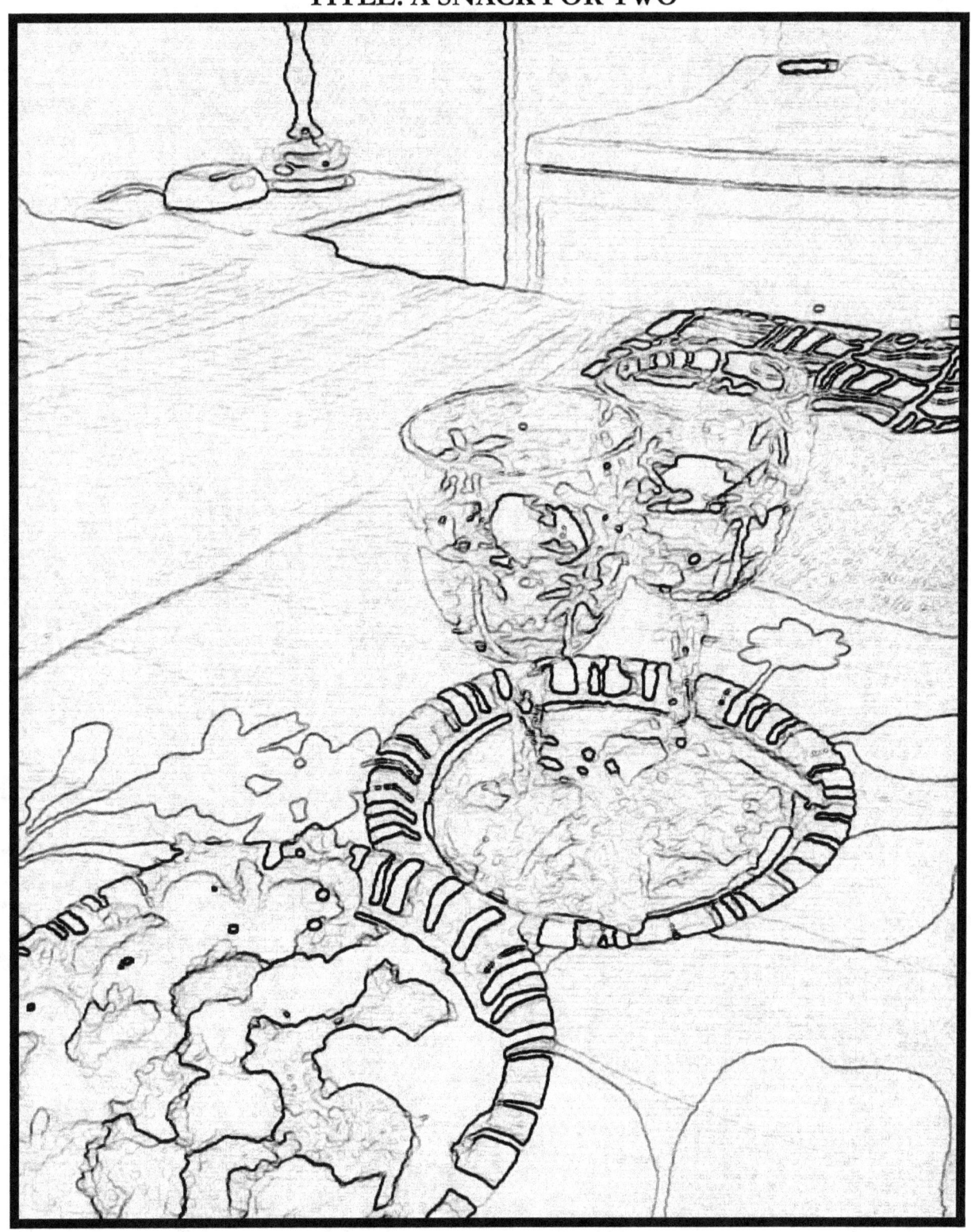

27

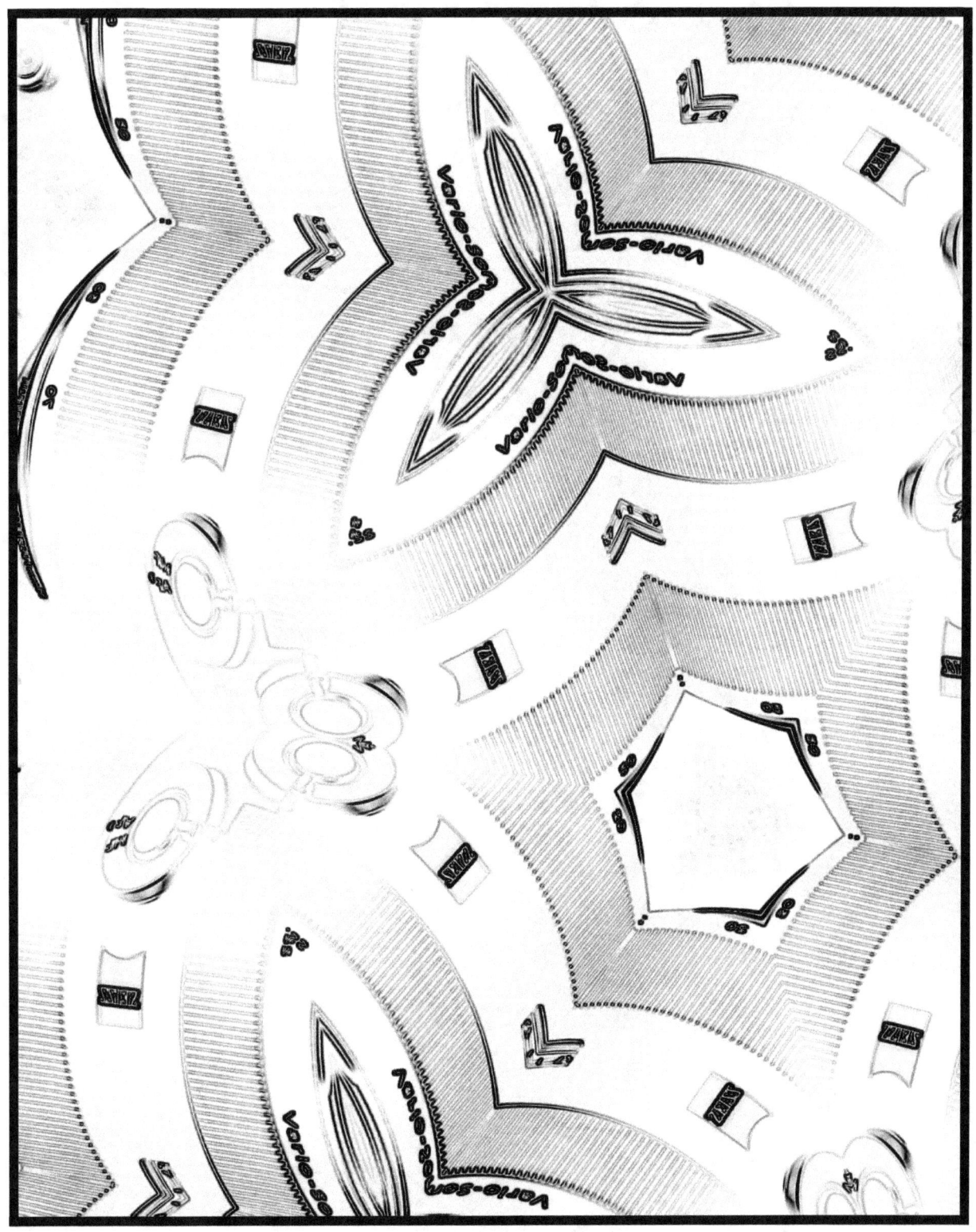

QUICK STRESS RELIEF
TITLE: PLAYFUL PUP

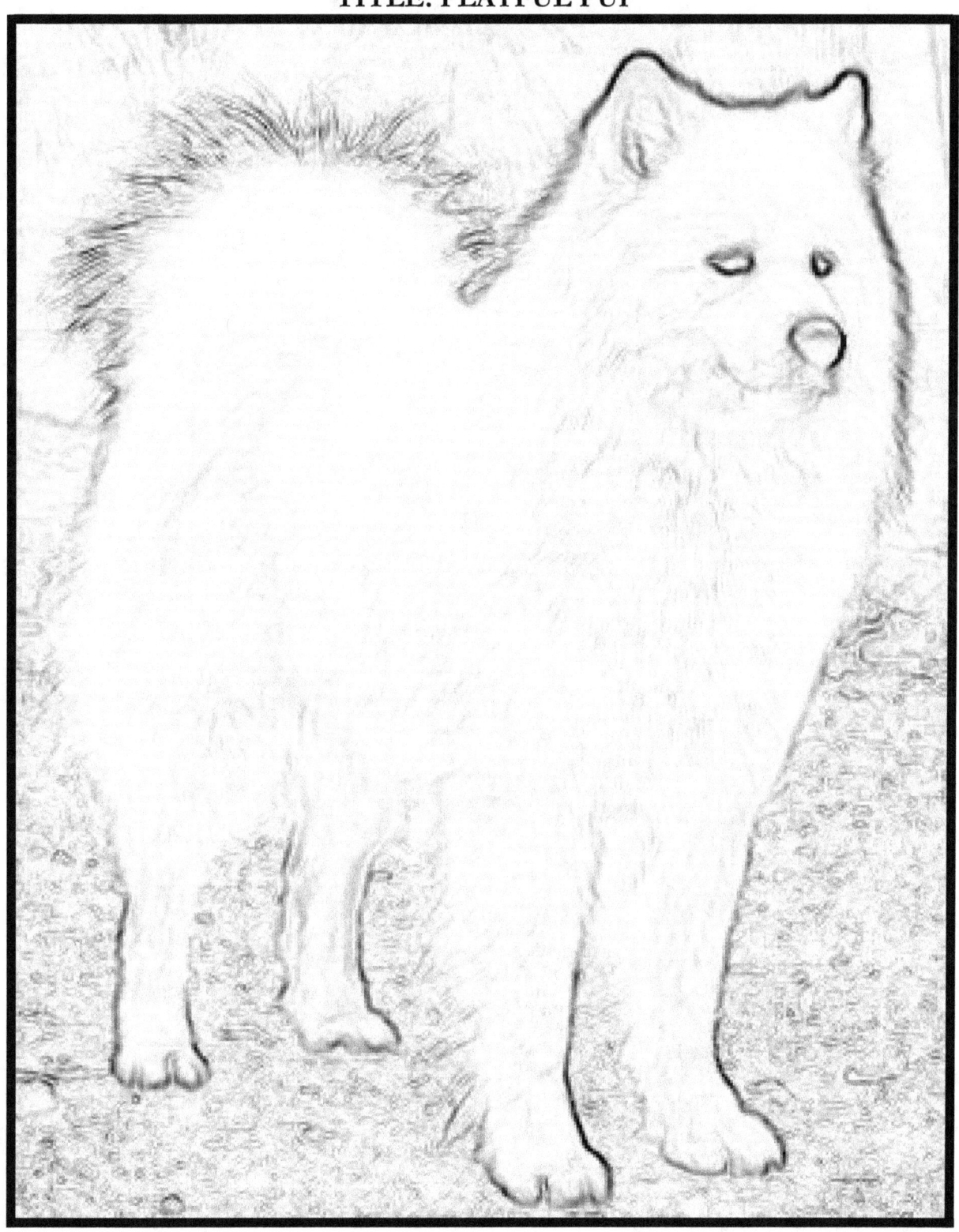

TITLE: DIAMONDS ARE A GIRLS BEST FRIEND

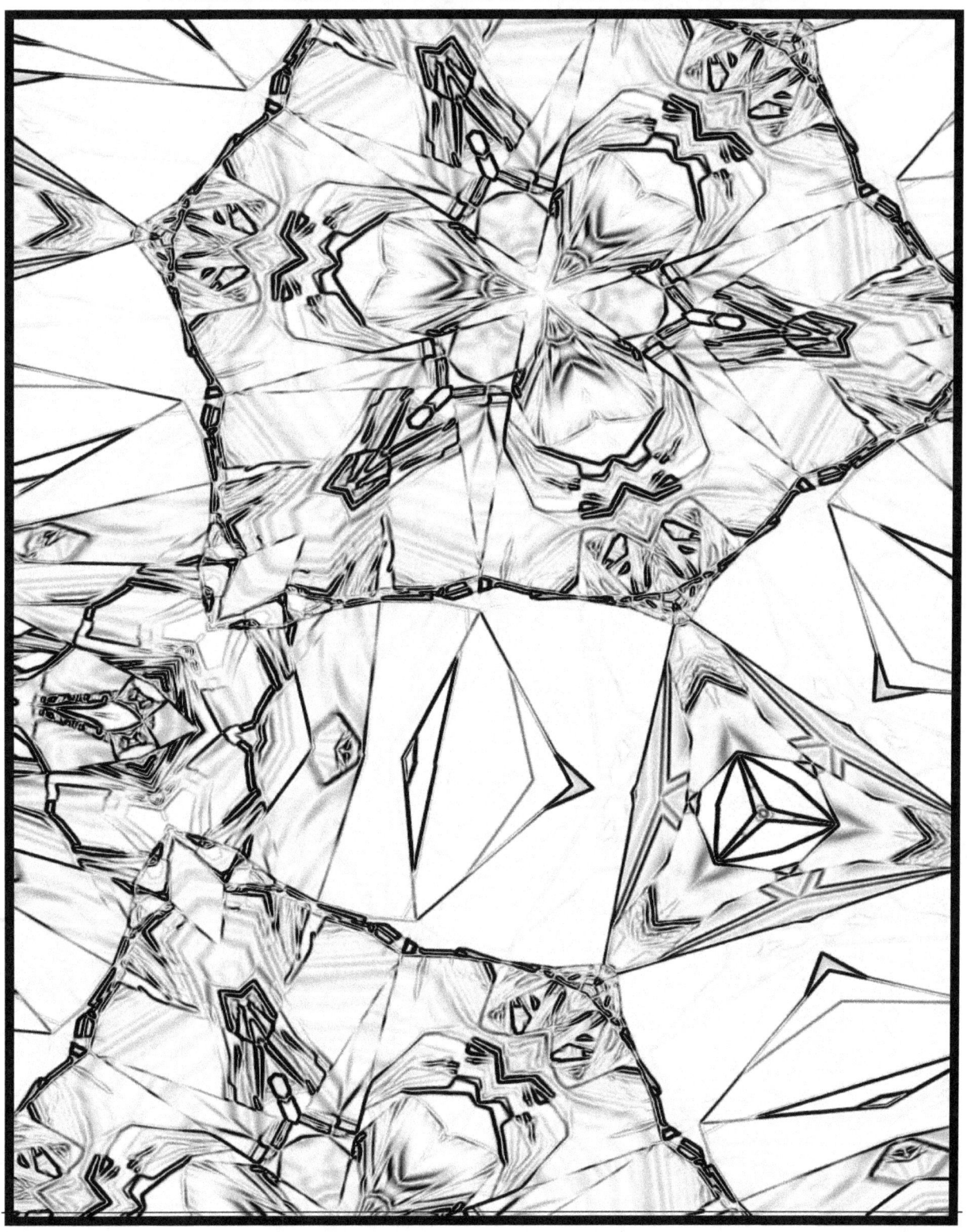

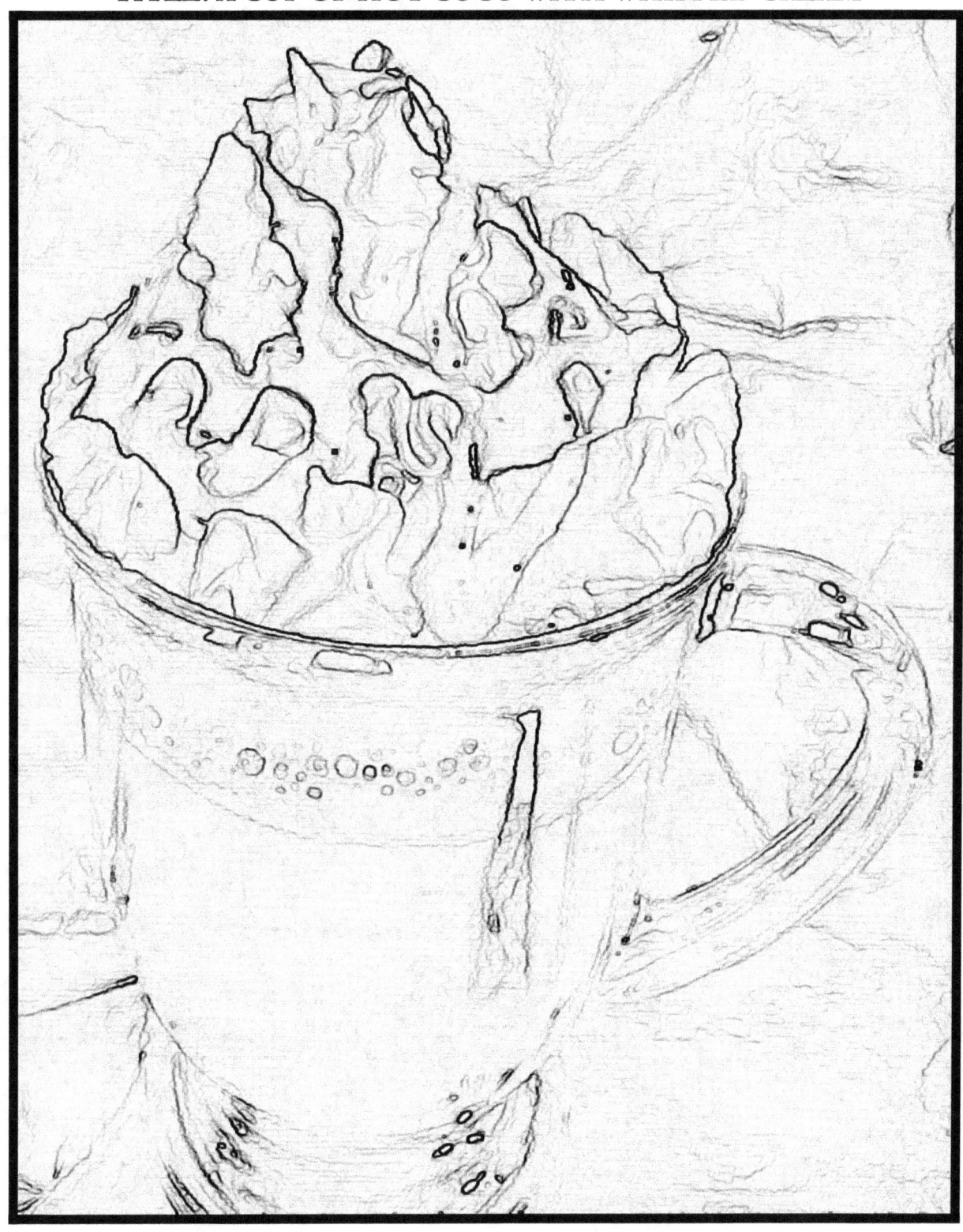

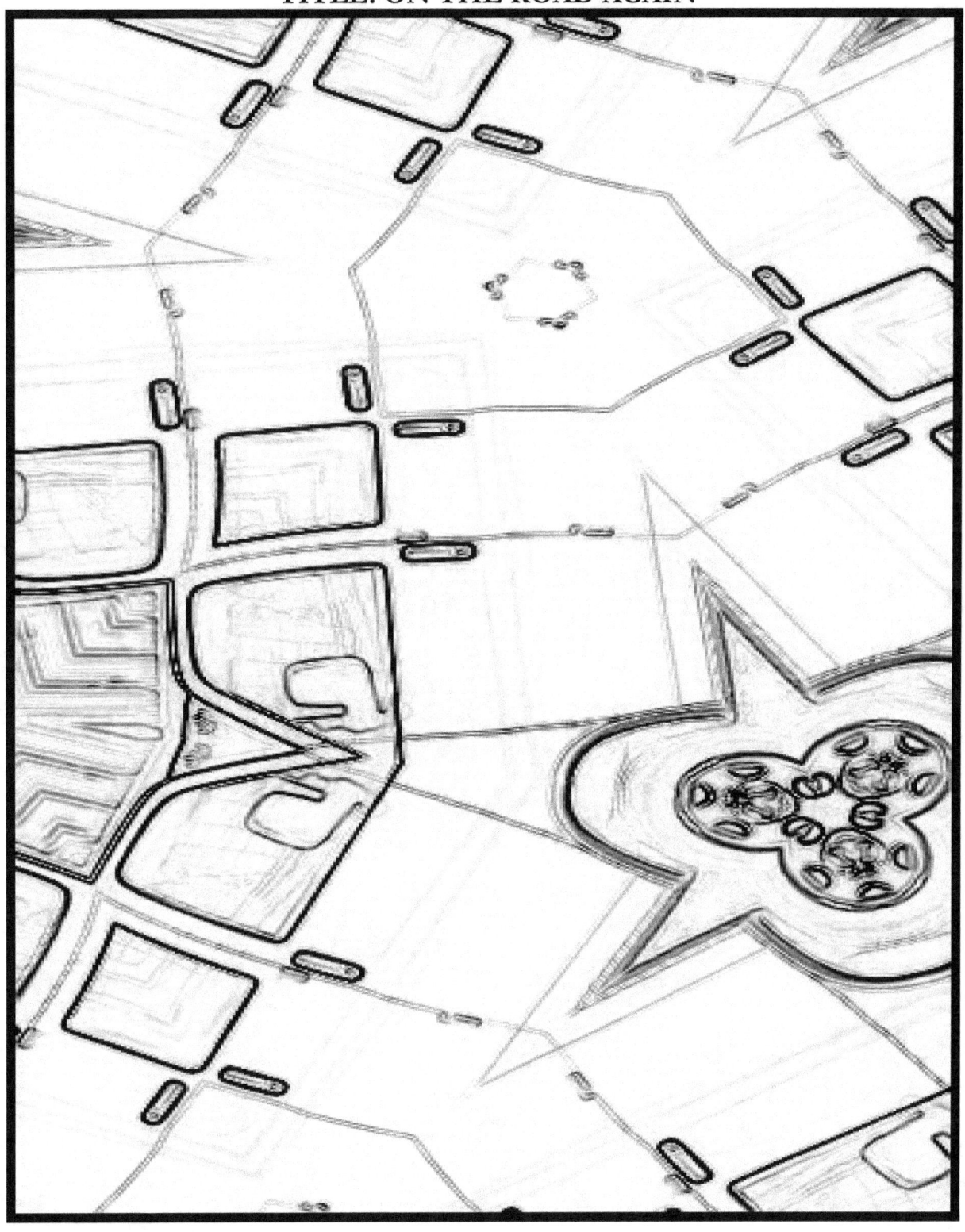

www.ingramcontent.com/pod-product-compliance
Lightning Source LLC
Chambersburg PA
CBHW081309180526
45170CB00007B/2633